"TOO MANY COOKS..."

and other proverbs

ILLUSTRATED BY

Maggie Kneen

GREEN TIGER PRESS
Published by Simon & Schuster
New York · London · Toronto · Sydney · Tokyo · Singapore

Birds of a feather flock together.

Many hands make light work.

Too many cooks spoil the broth.

If wishes were horses,
beggars would ride.

Never look a gift
horse in the mouth.

Don't put the cart before the horse.

You can lead a horse to water,
but you can't make it drink.
Don't lock the stable door
after the horse has bolted.

Look before you leap.
FENCE
1

He who hesitates is lost.

The best laid plans of mice and men oft go awry.

Waste not, want not.

A fool and his money are soon parted.

Half a loaf is better than none.

Don't judge a book by its cover.

Every cloud has
a silver lining.

Count your blessings.

Laugh and the world laughs with you . . .

Cry and you cry alone.

You can't teach an old dog new tricks.

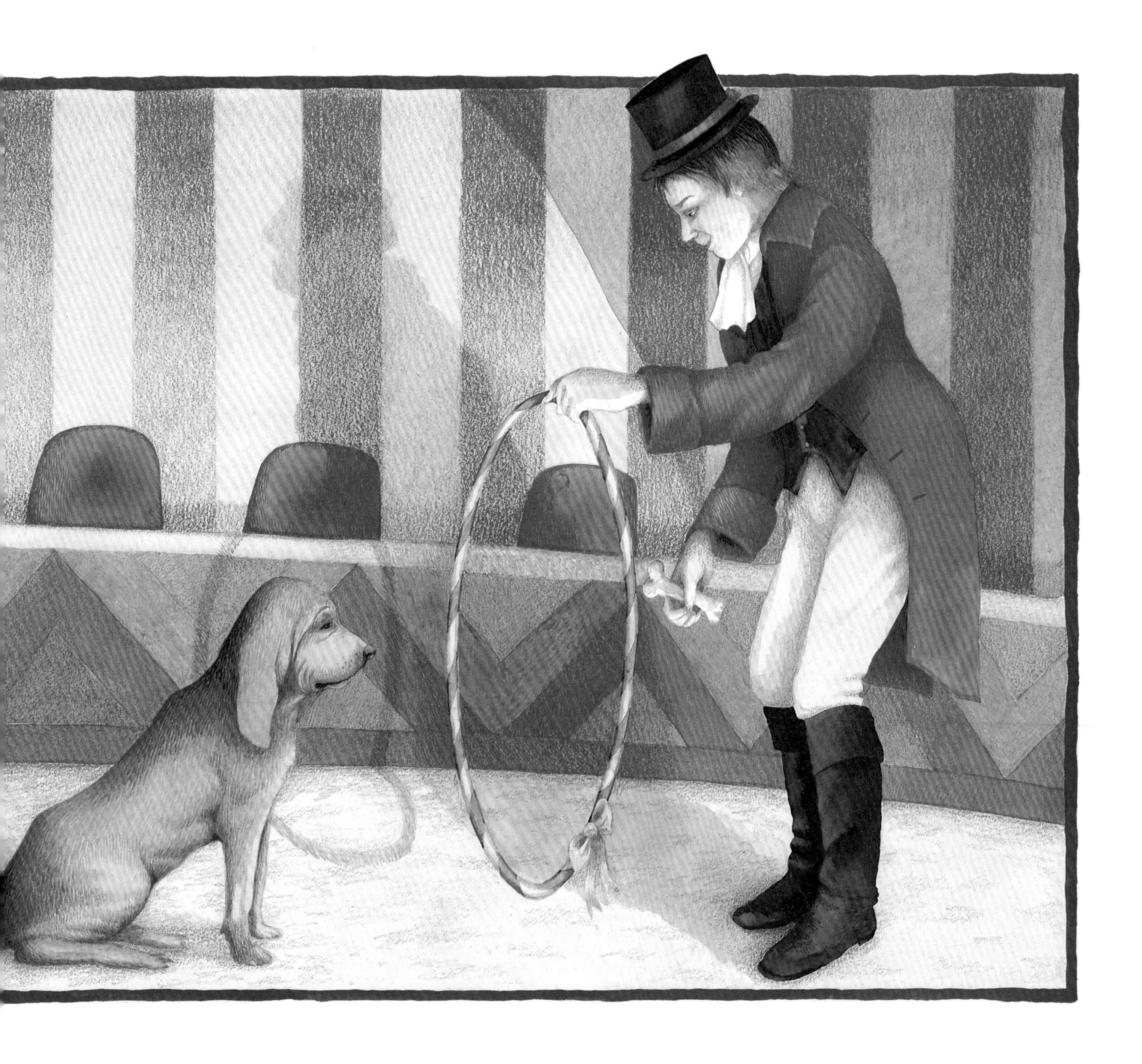

Once bitten, twice shy.

If at first you don't succeed, try, try again.

The early bird catches the worm.

A bird in the hand is worth two in the bush.

Don’t put all your eggs in one basket.

Don’t count your chickens before they hatch.

WHAT ARE PROVERBS?

Proverbs might be described as popular sayings that give advice. To be a proverb, a saying must become part of everyday language — part of the folk wisdom of a country. Its origin is usually forgotten and, in some cases, completely lost. Although many proverbs have a literal meaning, they can usually be applied to a wider range of situations.

•

Birds of a feather flock together.
People with the same interests often form groups or become friends.

Many hands make light work.
The more people there are to do a job, the more quickly it can be done.

Too many cooks spoil the broth.
If too many people try to do the same job at the same time, like making soup, they often make a mess of it.

If wishes were horses, beggars would ride.
If people could get what they wanted just by wishing, everyone's life would be very easy.

Never look a gift horse in the mouth.
Do not criticize something you have received as a gift. A horse's teeth can tell you its age, so if you are given a horse for nothing, you should not look at its teeth before accepting it.

You can lead a horse to water, but you can't make it drink.
You can try and persuade a person to share your views or do something you think is right for them, but you cannot force them to agree with you.

Don't put the cart before the horse.
Just as the horse pulls the cart, not the cart the horse, people should deal with jobs or events in the right order.

Don't lock the stable door after the horse has bolted.
It is useless to take precautions after an accident has happened when they should have been taken before.

Look before you leap.
Do not act in haste; always think carefully about what you're going to do before you do it.

He who hesitates is lost.
If you take too long to make up your mind about something, you may miss an opportunity that will never come again.

The best laid plans of mice and men oft go awry.
Nothing is perfect. However hard you try

to make sure that things will go smoothly, something may still go wrong.

Waste not, want not.

If you are careful with your money, you will be able to buy the things you need.

A fool and his money are soon parted.

Foolish people spend their money without thinking and soon they have none left.

Every cloud has a silver lining.

Every event, however bad, has its hopeful side — just as the dark cloud that hides the sun is ringed with silver and proves that the sun is still shining.

Half a loaf is better than none.

People should be grateful for what they receive, even though it may be less than they wanted or hoped for.

Count your blessings.

Things could be worse; be grateful for the things you have and do not always wish for more.

Don't judge a book by its cover.

Do not make up your mind about people, or things, just from the way they look — find out first what they are really like.

Laugh and the world laughs with you, cry and you cry alone.

Happy people make others feel good. A sad person makes other feel uncomfortable, so they tend to keep their distance.

You can't teach an old dog new tricks.

As people grow older, they are less able to understand new ideas and less willing to try new activities.

Once bitten, twice shy.

If people have had a nasty experience, they are reluctant to try the same thing again.

If at first you don't succeed, try, try again.

If you fail at something the first time, you should not give up. Have patience and continue trying until you can do the task.

The early bird catches the worm.

Those who arrive early get the best choice and do not miss any opportunities.

Don't put all your eggs in one basket.

Do not risk everything you have by putting it into a single venture. However well you have been advised, things can still go wrong.

A bird in the hand is worth two in the bush.

It is better to accept what you have than to let it go and hope to get something better later on.

Don't count your chickens before they hatch.

Never act on something good that you think may happen because it may not turn out as you imagine.